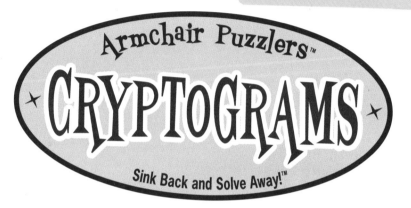

Armchair Puzzlers™
CRYPTOGRAMS

Sink Back and Solve Away!™

Maria Llull

UNIVERSITY
GAMES

Editorial Director: Erin Conley
Designers: Jeanette Miller, Lisa Yordy

Special thanks to Suzanne Cracraft, Lynn Gustafson, Courtney Hallum,
Audrey Haworth, Emily Jocson, Jennifer Ko, Cris Lehman, Bob Moog,
Tami Sartor, Nancy Spector and Mike Van Lonkhuysen
for their invaluable assistance!

Printed in China.

ISBN 1-57528-957-1

Table of Contents

Introduction

Pql hvicprxven cwuubla jz pqja srrd hrzpejz pql alhvlp pr lplvzeb irwpq. Rdei, pqep'a ez rklvapeplnlzp. Swp pqli evl e nleza pr dllcjzx irwpq jz irwv bjgl. Hwvjrwa?

Hwvjrajpi nleza "pql ywlap grv hrzpjzwrwa blevzjzx." Si hrzapezpbi blevzjzx, tl dllc rwv svejza irwzx ezf ehpjkl. J dzrt nezi clrcbl tqr fr hvicprxven cwuubla ezf pqli'vl ebb ea irwpqgwb ea acvjzx hqjhdlza ezf ea aqevc ea pehda. Pqli'vl ebar ebb vrhdlp ahjlzpjapapa ezf Zrslb Cvjul tjzzlva ezf Aqedlaclevlez ehprva. Ezf pqli rtl jp ebb pr hrwzpblaa qrwva aclzp arbkjzx hvicprxven cwuubla.

Jp'a irwv hwvjrajpi pqep tjbb fvjkl irw pr arbkl pql cwuubla jz pqja srrd. J qrcl irw qekl gwz – ezf vlnlnslv pr eccbi pqep hwvjrajpi pr irwv lklvifei bjgl!

Best wishes,
Maria Llull

4

Instructions

Cryptograms are coded puzzles that are solved by letter substitution. Each page has its own secret code to crack. Once you determine what the correct substitution is for a given letter, it is the same throughout the puzzle. For example, if you figure out that X=A, then every time "X" appears in the puzzle, it will equal "A."

This Cryptogram book is filled, brimming, packed with … yes, cryptograms! There are two different kinds: **Crypto Quotes** and **Crypto Families** … and you'll find that the Quotes are in some way (sometimes in a very remote way!) related to the Families. This connection may help you to solve the puzzle, but there are also Hints (pgs 86 – 87) if you need them.

5

Crypto Quotes

The quotes in this book are from movies, TV shows, books, celebrities, historical figures and song lyrics. Remember, the quotes are linked to the Crypto Families on the opposite page in some way!

Crypto Families

A group of 10 related items is listed in code under a subject title (i.e., "Beatles Songs"). Use the subject as a starting point to help you crack the code.

Crypto Quote

"M blyno Eykj Sojjyj, 'M wyj'n
dosmopo mj nko Doxnsoc, M elcn
dosmopo mj fo.' Hyyw rymjn
nkouo. Xqnou xss, ko ixc
Nko Ixsulc."

Qouumc Dlossou'c Wxg Yqq

6

Crypto Family
Beatles Songs

Jfao Uo Ef

Yfuoxnzcp

Cf Komjt

Nojxok Ysojxok

Noko Dfuoy xno Ybc

Jox Zx Ho

Tojjfv Ybhuwkzco

Xvzyx wce Ynfbx

Dfuo Xfpoxnok

Ozpnx Ewty a Voos

Crypto Quote

"Hjgrodllc wgb td dgldb

ymhl hawwdhhpaqqv cp vma

cbogqd cl qcid g zgwaay

wqdgbdf."

8

—Hmjocg Qmfdb

Crypto Family
Italian Dishes

Qruhwiccj

Mjhucayj

Vuyyioayj

Mudjaoj

Ouquhyu

Gjyiqcmayi

Hyavvwj

Ruyjyj

Ojyhejyj

Camcioojyj

9

Crypto Quote

"Szgkfy jwpk qo Spkvo Evznf

Cpqkqon jve p kepqo

Poy Q cpg jffwqon ofpewi pg jpyfy pg bi afpog.

Svssi klzbsfy p yqfgfw yvco

Azgk sfjvef qk epqofy

Klpk evyf zg pww klf cpi kv Ofc Vewfpog."

"Bf poy Svssi BhNff"

—Apoqg Avdwqo

10

Crypto Family
US State Capitals

Blfpro Btnz, Ohglxl

Nlsslalpphh, Ysrftxl

Ahshol, Kronlol

Dlnro Frcvh, Srctptlol

Kronqhsthf, Ghfkron

Plbflkhonr, Blstyrfotl

Arorscsc, Aliltt

Dtpklfw, Orfna Xlwrnl

Toxtlolqrstp, Toxtlol

Ehyyhfpro Btnz, Ktpprcft

Crypto Quote

"Cfrdr'z s ntaardrpbr hrckrrp qz.

Xmq cftpv cfr ormoer ma cftz espn rltzc

cm odmutnr xmq ktcf omztctmp. T cftpv xmqd

omztctmp rltzcz cm odmutnr cfmzr ormoer

ktcf adrrnmi. Spn T jm cm isvr zqdr

cfsc cfrx fsur tc."

Hdsurfrsdc

Crypto Family

'90s Best Picture Oscars®

Rwgqli zumd Zphbli

Waleuqwg Jlwnmk

Idwolislwel ug Hpbl

Mdl Iuhlgql pv mdl Hwaji

Jewbldlwem

Vpeelim Tnas

Ngvpetublg

Mumwguq

Mdl Lgthuid Swmulgm

Iqdugrhle'i Huim

13

Crypto Quote

"Nfgy O hoxmw mwuxwga orbxkcomoyp
uw Mgikya Iowq, O num mk sua O nuzdga
khh uya aoay'w ikrg suid hkx, zodg,
wnk qguxm. Wfgy O elmw zocga u zowwzg
uya iurg suid nowf u zkw rkxg bgxmky
wk kbgxuwg nowf."

—Sozz Rlxxuq

14

Crypto Family

Famous "Bills"

Esmmh olw Isu

Esmmh Yxhvojm

Esmm Fjowv

Esmmh Bzwm

Esmm Ymsaoza

Esmm Ncxxjh

Esmm Yzveh

Esmmsw Lzmsujh

Esmmh Eze Olzxaoza

Esmm Njlwx

Crypto Quote

"Wbzcdszcw sd obgrj wdbu vhsisit rbit

cibgtf abv dfc wdhvw db ebzc bgd,

hij dfci sd ohw isec. Sd ohw rsyc ngwd qcabvc

dfc wgi tbcw db qcj jboi bi dfc qhmbg.

Dfcvc ohw hrohmw h zsrrsbi wuhvyrcw

bi dfc ohdcv."

Abvvcwd Tgzu

Crypto Family
Constellations

Vlffjiksjl

Ybfl Tlqib

Kshlfyf

Ybfl Tjrib

Msbvywsf

Lrobitsol

Ibjir

Ksbfsyf

Hstjrj

lhjaalbjyf

Crypto Quote

Xspah: "Gwzzoqbazr, qk mlhm frxr kflk ysx

hsw ks qbfrxqk kfr ysxkwbr, hsw flir ks

mjrbe kfr orrarbe qb Lgsvqblgzr Vlbsx."

18

Gwzzoqbazr: "Kflk'm bs jxsgzrv. Q'ir

grrb zqiqbd qb lb lgsvqblgzr vlbbrx

lzz vh zqyr."

Kfr Gwzzoqbazr Mfso

Crypto Family
Cartoon Characters

Vsge Jmibjno

Lqrzpyvyggh Lnqof

Vqcj Vqooh

Vyswmj sof Vqeelysf

Vqppumozpy A. Innjy

Hncm Vysg

Kgyf Kpmoejenoy

Imrzyh Inqjy

Ypiyg Kqff

Vyeeh Vnnb

Crypto Quote

"Crlch pmlrlhd lr c yct oa yaj obfamib

klxd. Lx tam pmfft oaa wcht xcsafr,

tamf xfldhnr ylkk qd oaxm."

—Rblfkdt Xahi-Oaffdr

20

Crypto Family
Asian Foods

Xvmgmcpwhng

Xui Mauc

Gygac

Evd Mvdg

Mhnckuwc

Pave Lhcd

Ly Gay Xudpuwhg

Gxncdo Nvqqg

Gehhm udi Gvyn Gvyx

Mhlxynu

Crypto Quote

"M zxdmfhvaujhs, H fjhaq, hu dhqx m ujmzq.

Nve qavb? Hf jmu fv yvaufmafdn lvox pvzbmzr

vz hf rhxu. Mar H fjhaq bjmf bx'ox ivf va vez

jmaru hu m rxmr ujmzq."

Maahx Jmdd

Crypto Family

'70s Best Picture Oscars®

Foyyua

Ymv Eytah

Oaatv Monn

Ymv Pvvz Mlayvz

Ymv Hupxoymvz

Ymv Hupxoymvz Fozy TT

Zuqcs

Czoivz ke. Czoivz

Uav Xnvg Ukvz ymv Qlqcuu'e Avey

Ymv Xzvaqm Quaavqytua

Crypto Quote

"R xros otuiz'q xurku vuy uiltyq,

Wq wiz'q erwy rzo wq'i ztq zwlu.

R xros otuiz'q mrzouy rxx tkuy qvu ytta

Rzo jxtm tz itau tqvuy hbs'i owlu."

"Xblf Ju r Xros"

Hbsi rzo Otxxi

Crypto Family
Broadway Hits

Zafidjs jc dax Jzxwf

Gxe Skexwfmgxe

Dax Zwjyqnxwe

Dax Lkit fiy K

Bxed Ekyx Edjwp

Nfde

Naknftj

Tqpe fiy Yjgge

Dax Gkji Lkit

Xrkdf

Crypto Quote

"Mqf hwm oyrtp w mqyh wsyxu

Gerftom' grtwk nfwe...wto R, xtgyeuxtwufkn,

wv ytf yg uqymf skruqfertp roryum hqy berfo yt

Ydewq. R byxkot'u muyd vnmfkg."

— Ifttrgfe Wtrmuyt

Crypto Family
Oprah's Book Club Picks

Mct Okawkhpkkg Zaznt

Gdlrcmtf kv Vkfmlht

Cklwt kv Wdhg dhg Vkr

Mct Oankm'w Pavt

Wkhrw ah Kfgahdfu Mast

Mct Ctdfm kv a Pksdh

Rdo Efttq

Wct'w Ekst Lhgkht

Pcamt Kntdhgtf

Kht Clhgftg Utdfw kv Wknamlgt

Crypto Quote

"M qnui nyzntg qnsiv sqns vnok

Enoig Chkv. M'v ympi sh pmyy qmo."

— Gink Fhkkibt

Crypto Family
James Bond Movies

E Zniu pq e Gnxx

Wsqa Sljjne unpc Xqzi

Yni Edqpcis Yeo

Yneaqdyj esi Wqsizis

Xnzi edy Xip Yni

Ys. Dq

Mqxywndmis

Qfpqkljjo

Pci Xnzndm Yeoxnmcpj

Pci Jko Ucq Xqziy Ai

Crypto Quote

"Askb wez lhg kezpz wez buvewx hpz vhg

Hba wez xyb xeubzx ahufg sb wez qsybwhub wsi

U wssj h wpui sb h xhufubv xeui

Hba kezb U pzhdeza Rhqhudh U qhaz h xwsi."

"Rhqhudh Ohpzkzff"

—Ehppg Lzfhosbwz

30

Crypto Family
Earth's Islands

Nlccsbfl

Sljy

Dsbmas

Pbalr Dbkrlkm

Lmrkpyl

Zyabrs Bkfs

Nlulpliflb

Pbaamclmu

Vlnlkfl

Dabnyul

Crypto Quote

"J eap qrf reqfs bpm sjnf qrfxf.

Ke dew ubp gxfqqd zwur kbd qrbq zd

sjlf jk sjyf Zepegesd."

32

Qae Affyk Peqjuf

Crypto Family
Board Games

Nfdsg Bfds

Nbot

Wpdphpbg

Karirfb Hoazork

Kmtdkg Uotzkrpdz

Znafjjbt

Jfbstasfzy

Nyoktz fds Bfsstaz

Kyt Xfwt pq Brqt

Hrnkrpdfag

Crypto Quote

"R'j zgqb xvunp

Ezge vrez erlb

Ezufszex ut huf

Vufoj obgqb lh zbgj.

R vgx vnups

Gpj R trpj

Dfxe upb ezrps

Lgwbx lb tunsbe."

"Nbj, Nbj Vrpb"

—Pbro Jrglupj

Crypto Family
Types of Wine

Tlxspkx

Mlqffo

Clxkq Vxpnspjqz

Wqfzhk

Tlsfjhppso

Yxphk Phxf

Tlsazxm

Tsaqfpqk Mseuxbphp

Yhfk

Fhmq

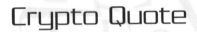

"Ajgvx, kxr'jg dk xhvgj zjxmbgj

cov P hxwg kxr, zrm vxo'm gwgj mcqg

epvge ypmb cokxog clcpoem

mbg acdphk clcpo. Gwgj."

36

Mbg Lxvacmbgj

Crypto Family
AI Pacino Movies

Zubtd hn l Ihslt

Zulvnlub

Pebtplvvj Pebt Vhzz

Zbvmouh

Nvltqob ltc Ahyttj

Ulveodh'z Ilj

Dyb Phcnldybv

Lfdyhv! Lfdyhv!

Zbl hn Ehwb

Ltj Powbt Zftclj

37

Crypto Quote

"Ua u jyer aquj,

X cuzn qiy xoaqxoeqa:

X iuoq qy cuzn wbo uok X

iuoq qy ecuopn qcn iyjtk.

X cuzn u ecuoen qy ky hyqc."

— Hyoy

Crypto Family

Musicians Known By One Name

Hrofkkr

Ivtn

Utiz

Tkpr

Ufkf

Thbkth

Gxbkl

Uyfnz

Ytetw

Grot

Crypto Quote

"Eqjm B exi x icxss dhv bm Lxmixi,

x rwbjmg hr cbmj xmg B ejma rbiqbmn.

B ahsg qbc B exmajg ah dj x wjxs Cxfhw

Sjxnyj Dxijdxss tsxvjw, x njmybmj

twhrjiibhmxs sblj Qhmyi Exnmjw. Cv

rwbjmg ixbg aqxa qj'g sblj ah dj

Twjibgjma hr aqj Ymbajg Iaxaji.

Mjbaqjw hr yi nha hyw ebiq."

— Gebnqa G. Jbijmqhejw

Crypto Family

Major League Baseball Home Towns

Leyytwfsvc

Tbx Jsbxoetor

Agysrey

Ty. Mrfet

Oexoexxbye

Crftyrx

Xgh Ursp Oeyu

Bymbxyb

Tgbyymg

Wrtyrx

Crypto Quote

"Mu iar fmte umtjk dxi wdx nvr tdi n bnjw,

wdx ymbb lr infrt id iar Idyrv du Bdtjdt,

yarvr wdxv arnj ymbb lr pxi duu nk

n ynvtmte id diarv zvrkxgzixdxk

ubdyrv emvbk!"

Gw Unmv Bnjw

Crypto Family
'60s Best Picture Ocsars®

Jmogqubq tv Mgmilm

Oqpe Plfq Petgn

Sn Vmlg Jmfn

M Smu vtg Mjj Pqmptup

Ezq Mxmgesque

Ets Wtuqp

Ezq Ptauf tv Saplb

Tjlkqg!

Slfulyze Btoitn

Lu ezq Zqme tv ezq Ulyze

Crypto Quote

"Vy fwx'a aone ohwia oxzakdxs

cymbwxon. Vy rofy o miny ohwia akoa.

D fwx'a exwv kdb xory, vkoa ky fwyb

wm yloganz vkymy ky ndqyb, bw da

vdnn hy myonnz yobz aw bawc

byydxs kdr, hygoiby D'r xwa."

Zwi'qy Swa Rodn

Crypto Family
Email Providers

zzz.byclsweqd.qbl

zzz.yiw.aio

zzz.qblvaykb.aio

zzz.ubcetiq.aio

zzz.rxqi.aio

zzz.nysii.aio

zzz.ovq.aio

zzz.siloyew.aio

zzz.fzbvl.aio

zzz.aiokxvbcub.aio

Crypto Quote

"E'g wepa sna yea naksag kmg E gxm's

vkms sna eia izakq xm sxy, E vkms es

xm sna lega. Kmg E'g wepa lszkvjazzh

emlsakg xd bkmewwk ed hxo nkba es.

Ed mxs, snam mx eia izakq, rols vneyyag

izakq, jos xmwh ed es'l zakw. Ed es'l xos xd

sna ikm, snam mxsnemt."

Vnam Nkzzh Qas Lkwwh...

Crypto Family
Ice Cream Flavors

Rlye Hqlm

Hqdhdfcev

Kdhub Kdcs

Hddulvp cys Hkvcr

Wxeevk Mvhcy

Nkvyhq Jcylffc

Hdhdyxe

Pekcgwvkkb

Yvdmdflecy

Hdnnvv

Crypto Quote

"Umh shqpsrpcfh umojb pcatu Xmprhxihpsh

ox umpu mh shpffw ox lhsw baag,

oj xiouh ae pff umh ihaifh zma

xpw mh ox lhsw baag."

— Sachsu Bsplhx

Crypto Family

The Works of Shakespeare

G Khzdckkab Lhtfq'd Zbagk   *Bukau glz Scvhaq*

Kgrmaqf   *Uqfavvu*

Qfa Rukazn uj Abbubd   *Kcrf Gzu gmucq Luqfhlt*

Qfa Qgkhlt uj qfa Dfbax   *Fgkvaq*

Qfa Kabbn Xhwad uj Xhlzdub

Qfa Qxu Talqvakal uj Wabulg

Crypto Quote

"Sfl mefv, rc'k p kypha Iaftia'k dptaeck

qrqe'c iac qrjftxaq cyrtcs saptk pif.

Ya xfloq ypja zaae efthpo."

Karenaoq

Crypto Family
Famous "Georges"

Qudequ Jontbur

Qudequ Tbeeokdi

Qudequ P. Vfkt

Qudequ Gdeujbi

Qudequ Nrddiuw

Vdw Qudequ

Qudequ J. Ndtbi

Qudequ Rfnbk

Nfeodfk Qudequ

Quiuebr Qudequ K. Sbccdi

Crypto Quote

"E'c luekl nu xdabj juq iux
fdnxbjekl cd; E'c luekl nu lerd ngbn
fxbek ui juqxt b kdy gucd ek ngd
tvqmm ui ngd Ixbkvdktndek cuktndx."

Guqtd ui Ixbkvdktndek

Crypto Family
Scary Movies

Jfbaloxig uj Gmo Tliggl

Axmmuqggj

Rifbal Jfbal

Lag Lgdxt Zaxfjtxq Oxttxzig

Jfbal ur lag Mfpfjb Ygxy

Tzigxo

Lag Tfdla Tgjtg

Lag Gduizftl

Stvzau

Lag Ohoov

Crypto Quote

"Ehhs ewxc, fz cho xhg'i zfgx

w uwaafi dfij efktifys wbotfgv,

ijqg cho wgx F jwrq ghijfg' ih twc

ih qwyj hijqu!"

— Aovt Aoggc

Crypto Family
Cosmetics
Manufacturers

Mozx

Vzdamv

Cmdu Hmu

Wvyxynla

Iakrzdm

Wzoad Bydv

Cmusavvyxa

Vmxwzca

Wrmxav

Ldsmx Eawmu

Crypto Quote

"Pidz d xwo ijdtz W idkj,

Zij xjzzjt zn unkj enl pwzi.

Uwzzuj Tjc Twcwvo Innc,

Jkjv xdc pnukjy adv xj onnc.

W'uu zte zn qjjs ydzwyrwjc,

Blyz zn pduq xe enlt ywcj.

Gdexj enl'uu yjj ziwvoy ge pde,

Xjrntj pj ojz zn Otdvcgd'y sudaj."

"Uwzzuj Tjc Twcwvo Innc"

—Ydg zij Yidg dvc zij Sidtdniy

Crypto Family
Children's Fairy Tales

Qnll wh Siirl

Xnuqjalrwarlewh

Fdhlja dhk Pxjrja

Riu Rfnus

Cdge dhk rfj Sjdhlrdae

Rfj Qxwhgjll dhk rfj Qjd

Rfnusjawhd

Awrraj Xjk Xwkwhp Fiik

Sjdnrz dhk rfj Sjdlr

Rfj Yxip Qxwhgj

57

Crypto Quote

"Rciql bhgg nycq xkiqh jyjhuvx. Vahn

iqh gezh cufcv leijyulx. Lexfiql vahj

iul vaheq migch begg uhmhq dh zuybu.

Ejkqymh vahj iul vahn begg

dhfyjh vah dqeravhxv rhjx eu i cxhtcg geth."

— Qigka Bigly Hjhqxyu

58

Crypto Family
Jewelry Gems

Hnvp

Vlgbqudb

Msvlhtm

Lvpvfqsbg

Vljgy

Avytgb

Ywju

Jpwg Bhnve

Ovmg

Htui

Crypto Quote

"Ib uqvg cqmm nvlbtv zmm gwv

ezg enbl xbhn kbux kvfzhjv gwv knzqi

qj vigqnvmx ezg. Cqgwbhg z knzqi

xbh lqrwg mbbs rbbu, khg zmm xbh

fbhmu ub qj nhi ebn dhkmqf beeqfv."

— Rvbnrv Kvniznu Jwzc

Crypto Family
Diet Fads

Ldowa Yukea Hxuw

Tklwucxbq wau Mdbu

Qckguzcoxw Hxuw

Ukw Cxqaw zdc fdoc Wfgu

Hc. Kwixbl' Hxuw

Lekclhkru Hxuw

Gcxwxixb Hxuw

Yusucrf Axrrl Hxuw

61

Ekyykqu Ldog Hxuw

Bukbhuc-Waxb: Ukw Rxiu k Eksutkb

Crypto Quote

"Il [Lcpjh] kvh vh ojt vh bil kircl

yrxubsd jbhlcz, vh ojt vh bil kircl qslvf.

Il nxhb lforqjlq bil lhhluyl rz jb vuq il

kvh ju frsbvc yrfovb kjbi bil bijut.

Urbijut kjcc lpls bvwl bil gcvyl

rz bivb txd."

— Osxyl Hgsjuthbllu

Crypto Family
Elvis Presley Songs

"Oula Va Sadkac"

"Gca Jum Oudafuva Sudtwys?"

"Yumdk Kuw"

"Fmfrtitumf Vtdkf"

"G Otssoa Oaff Iudlacfgstud"

"Yagcsncagq Yusao"

"Kud's Na Icmao"

"Pgtoyumfa Cuiq"

"Nmcdtdw Oula"

"Goo Fyuuq Mr"

Crypto Quote

"Rgcr tck lxngr rgyly xu tf zlbrgyl cks

xo gy sbyuk'r nyr rb ecrdg *Qybqjy'u Dbilr*

xk czbir rgxlrf uydbksu, gy'u nbkkc rglbe

c oxr lxngr gyly bk fbil qbldg. Kbe fbi

dck gyjq ty bl fbi dck urcks rgyly

cks ecrdg xr gcqqyk."

Lcxk Tck

Crypto Family
'80s Best Picture Oscars®

Bwsdklwt Uqbuaq

Hlksyd

Bvf bc Lcwdzl

Ualfbbk

Wldk Xlk

Zylwdbfp bc Cdwq

Fqwxp bc Qksqlwxqkf

Lxlsqvp

Fyq Alpf Qxuqwbw

Swdmdkh Xdpp Sldpt

65

Crypto Quote

"Hk hwrmsx fnafkj djsp rw jfk,

'Rms wnpsx kwd vsr, rms isrrsx

kwd vsr, dgnsjj kwd'xs f ifgfgf.'"

Vwnpsg Vzxnj

Crypto Family
Tropical Fruit

Vtstst

Tdfktaf

Xqshtxxwh

Xtzzqfs Mpoqj

Rqiq

Xtxtut

Ntsbf

Botdt

Xfnhbptstjh

Xtixti

Crypto Quote

"G zniwhc vdjdk xdds r hdudvc.

Gs'z rharmz cgzrqqigvsgvu, hgfd snd sgxd

G xds Lgu Lgkc rs snd God Orqrcdz:

nd'z vis zi lgu."

Aghh & Ukrod

Crypto Family

Sesame Street® Characters

Rbwanl ldb Swfj

Znj Znwc

Bkaf

Gkpyncf Skpanujf

Yffrnb Afuhlbw

Jwfibw

Fhypw ldb Jwfqyd

Zbwl

Bwunb

Yfqul ifu Yfqul

Crypto Quote

"Epi wxle bxaiychr wnt mt epi

Htmeiv Leneil ml Byilmvite Tmzxt.

Oxh'ji pinyv xc pmw?"

Nrr epi Byilmvite'l Wit

Crypto Family
U.S. Presidents

Bnhbibd Gepwcgp

Thcyzh Wgzyzgbpj

Tzhbgj Lchj

Uizcjchz Hcckzyzgu

Ocip L. Xzppzjs

Tzchtz Mbkieptucp

Oedds Wbhuzh

Abwibhs Ubsgch

Wizkuzh B. Bhuivh

Vgskkzk K. Thbpu

Crypto Quote

"Bn'c vgttd lqjt ojaomj csd,

'B eat'n nqbtz Wgmbs mbzjc pj.'

Qatjd, bv B eat'n mbzj dag,

dag'kj iabti na ztal shagn bn."

72

— Wgmbs Kahjknc

Crypto Family
Julia Roberts Movies

Fvddm Bikjzmyif

Bg Qdfv Nhydjl'f Sdllyjk

Hcjisig Qhyld

Uzza

Fmddryjk syvu vud Djdbg

Vud Rdmywij Qhydn

Rhdvvg Szbij

Nmivmyjdhf

Dhyj Qhzwazoywu

Bgfvyw Ryeei

Crypto Quote

"Yfi awziplvplyc vs kfvkvnbyi,

dvyf svp fibnyf bjr jvwplafoijy,

tlnn avvj hlxi ly yfi aboi zpisipijki

vxip yib bjr kvssii lj Boiplkb

tflkf ly fba lj Azblj."

— Yfvoba Qissipavj

74

Crypto Family
Chocolate Cravings

Lcggstk

Sjm Jimqo

Jqtgv Rqi

Obcyym

Xbtgcm

Ribhtsm

Jqdm

Picxxfm

Nbp Jbjbq

Nbp Xcgkm

Crypto Quote

"L yrdu puzz oyrf zlm asfoyz

os pldu. Oyu Irksflz gupludu oyuq fuun

r yjarf zrbvlclbu sv oyulv lzprfn lz tslft

os zlfh lfos oyu sburf. Oyuq yrdu r alfuvrp

oyro qsjv croyuv irfoz zs yu ylvun au

os purk lfos oyulv dspbrfs."

Xsu Duvzjz oyu Dspbrfs

Crypto Family
Earth's Volcanoes

Rg. Puhurlcklon

Rg. Dgcl

Sdjuh'e Gnmdo

Rg. Vnns

Tlolybguc

Rg. Qbku

Rg. Jdebjube

Rg. Eg. Vdhdce

Rg. Hleedc

Polplgnl

Crypto Quote

"La icd pslhv pstp Kluv Etbbwm

qloo rploo gw xclhb psw qscow

mcuv rptm pslhb tp tbw alapi,

qwoo, pswh, icd tmw rcmwoi,

rcmwoi klrptvwh."

Tokcrp Atkcdr

Crypto Family
Rolling Stones Songs

Nypz Fykqolz

Pnbxi Qyrln

Lirdk

Rdaak Qvkwfkn

Pklqf bm Pynoki

Qflnf Ak Yb

Yiokn Az Fvyap

Vbigz Fbig Xbaki

Qzahlfvz mbn fvk Okudw

(D Jli'f Rkf Ib) Qlfdqmljfdbi

Crypto Quote

"Kasj wyg tsaze'q eggngqw sdgfr,

Kasj tfp estr ugzst, Kasj estr cr wyg

jle tygag wyg eggn-ecmgaq bs,

Kasj estr cr wyg jcag fre wyg jldx

fre wyg jlax, C jcbyw dfwdy qsjg

kcqy tys fag fzz bscrb,

'BZLAX!'"

JdGzzcbsw'q Nssz

— Ea. Qglqq

Crypto Family
Children's Authors

Peanmog Xguzew

Dgpvuj Xumowgk

Zn. Xgaxx

Ksg Hnvksgnx Cnmpp

Nmosenz Xoennj

Y. W. Nvtdmuc

Deane Muceddx Tmdzgn

Lneuw D. Heap

Pezgdgmug D'gucdg

Nvedz Zesd

Crypto Quote

"Z rfd fdtmb ny fgn rkmc Z gyvubc'n fgn.

Z rfd fdtmb ny dzch *Ivcce Ifgm* rkmc

Z gyvubc'n dzch, fcb ny bfcgm rznk

Ijmb Fdnfzjm rkmc Z gyvubc'n bfcgm

— fcb ny by fuu tzcbd yi nkzchd Z rfdc'n

wjmwfjmb iyj. Nkmc Z njzmb uztm pfb

ny gywm rznk zn."

— Fvbjme Kmwqvjc

Crypto Family
Audrey Hepburn Movies

Rxggp Rwuc

Vp Rwot Qwlp

Qznc og jmc Wrjctgzzg

Wqswpf

Swoj xgjoq Lwti

Etcwirwfj wj Jorrwgp'f

Fwetogw

Swt wgl Acwuc

Tzeog wgl Vwtowg

Tzvwg Mzqolwp

Crypto Quote

"Nm pze fgi jektp irzeqa bz afdi

jndiy nr Ufgnc fc f pzerq wfr,

bair haigidig pze qz mzg bai gicb

zm pzeg jnmi nb cbfpc hnba pze,

mzg Ufgnc nc f wzdifsji mifcb."

— Igricb Aiwnrqhfp

84

Crypto Family

Countries & Their Capitals

Vihwoh, Bgiop

Dwlbbjtb, Djtxolv

Piowado, Rjpfi

Hldtop, Owjtiph

Dlhigjbs, Elpxiwf

Giwob, Zwipmj

Djocopx, Meopi

Vipoti, Geotoggopjb

Pjn Hjteo, Ophoi

Ejtbopro, Zoptiph

Hints: Crypto Quotes

Hints: Crypto Families

87

Solutions: Crypto Quotes

Page 6 "I quote John Lennon, 'I don't believe in the Beatles, I just believe in me.' Good point there. After all, he was The Walrus."
Ferris Bueller's Day Off

Page 8 "Spaghetti can be eaten most successfully if you inhale it like a vacuum cleaner." — Sophia Loren

Page 10 "Busted flat in Baton Rouge, waiting for a train, And I was feeling nearly as faded as my jeans. Bobby thumbed a diesel down just before it rained, That rode us all the way to New Orleans." "Me and Bobby McGee"
—Janis Joplin

Page 12 "There's a difference between us. You think the people of this land exist to provide you with position. I think your position exists to provide those people with freedom. And I go to make sure that they have it."
Braveheart

Page 14 "When I first started improvising at Second City, I was so bad I walked off and didn't come back for, like, two years. Then I just lived a little and came back with a lot more person to operate with." — Bill Murray

Page 16 "Sometimes it would stop raining long enough for the stars to come out, and then it was nice. It was like just before the sun goes to bed down on the bayou. There was always a million sparkles on the water." *Forrest Gump*

Page 18 Rocky: "Bullwinkle, it says here that for you to inherit the fortune, you have to spend the weekend in Abominable Manor."
Bullwinkle: "That's no problem. I've been living in an abominable manner all my life."
The Bullwinkle Show

Page 20 "Asian cuisine is a way to wok through life. If you curry too many favors, your friends will be tofu." — Shirley Fong-Torres

Page 22 "A relationship, I think, is like a shark. You know? It has to constantly move forward or it dies. And I think what we've got on our hands is a dead shark." *Annie Hall*

Page 24 "A lady doesn't leave her escort, it isn't fair and it's not nice. A lady doesn't wander all over the room and blow on some other guy's dice." "Luck Be a Lady" *Guys and Dolls*

Page 26 "She was doing a show about *Friends'* final year... and I, unfortunately, am one of those blithering idiots who cried on *Oprah*. I couldn't stop myself." — Jennifer Aniston

Page 28 "I have always hated that damn James Bond. I'd like to kill him." — Sean Connery

Page 30 "Down the bay where the nights are gay, And the sun shines daily on the mountain top, I took a trip on a sailing ship and when I reached Jamaica I made a stop."
"Jamaica Farewell" —Harry Belafonte

Solutions: Crypto Quotes

Page 32 "I own the hotel and live there. So you can pretty much say that my life is like Monopoly." *Two Weeks Notice*

Page 34 "I'd have sworn that with time thoughts of you would leave my head. I was wrong and I find just one thing makes me forget." "Red, Red Wine" — Neil Diamond

Page 36 "Fredo, you're my older brother and I love you, but don't ever take sides with anyone against the family again. Ever."
The Godfather

Page 38 "As a rock star, I have two instincts: I want to have fun, and I want to change the world. I have a chance to do both." —Bono

Page 40 "When I was a small boy in Kansas, a friend of mine and I went fishing. I told him I wanted to be a real Major League Baseball player, a genuine professional like Honus Wagner. My friend said that he'd like to be President of the United States. Neither of us got our wish." —Dwight D. Eisenhower

Page 42 "If the king finds out you are not a lady, you will be taken to the Tower of London where your head will be cut off as a warning to other presumptuous flower girls!" *My Fair Lady*

Page 44 "We don't talk about anything personal. We made a rule about that. I don't know his name, what he does or exactly where he lives, so it will be really easy to stop seeing him, because I'm not." *You've Got Mail*

Page 46 "I'd like the pie heated and I don't want the ice cream on top, I want it on the side. And I'd like strawberry instead of vanilla if you have it. If not, then no ice cream, just whipped cream, but only if it's real. If it's out of the can, then nothing." *When Harry Met Sally…*

Page 48 "The remarkable thing about Shakespeare is that he really is very good, in spite of all the people who say he is very good." — Robert Graves

Page 50 "You know, it's a shame George's parents didn't get divorced thirty years ago. He could have been normal." *Seinfeld*

Page 52 "I'm going to repay you for betraying me; I'm going to give that brain of yours a new home in the skull of the Frankenstein monster." *House of Frankenstein*

Page 54 "Look lady, if you don't find a rabbit with lipstick amusing, then you and I have nothin' to say to each other!" — Bugs Bunny

Solutions: Crypto Quotes

Page 56 "What a big heart I have, the better to love you with. Little Red Riding Hood, Even bad wolves can be good. I'll try to keep satisfied, Just to walk by your side. Maybe you'll see things my way, Before we get to Grandma's place." "Little Red Riding Hood" —Sam the Sham and the Pharaohs

Page 58 "Guard well your spare moments. They are like uncut diamonds. Discard them and their value will never be known. Improve them and they will become the brightest gems in a useful life." — Ralph Waldo Emerson

Page 60 "No diet will remove all the fat from your body because the brain is entirely fat. Without a brain, you might look good, but all you could do is run for public office." — George Bernard Shaw

Page 62 "He [Elvis] was as big as the whole country itself, as big as the whole dream. He just embodied the essence of it and he was in mortal combat with the thing. Nothing will ever take the place of that guy." — Bruce Springsteen

Page 64 "That man right there is my brother and if he doesn't get to watch *People's Court* in about thirty seconds, he's gonna throw a fit right here on your porch. Now you can help me or you can stand there and watch it happen." *Rain Man*

Page 66 "My mother always used to say, 'The older you get, the better you get, unless you're a banana.'" *Golden Girls*

Page 68 "I should never meet a legend. It's always disappointing, like the time I met Big Bird at the Ice Capades: he's not so big." *Will & Grace*

Page 70 "The most powerful man in the United States is President Nixon. You've heard of him?" *All The President's Men*

Page 72 "It's funny when people say, 'I don't think Julia likes me.' Honey, if I don't like you, you're going to know about it." — Julia Roberts

Page 74 "The superiority of chocolate, both for health and nourishment, will soon give it the same preference over tea and coffee in America which it has in Spain." — Thomas Jefferson

Page 76 "I have less than six months to live. The Waponis believe they need a human sacrifice or their island is going to sink into the ocean. They have a mineral that your father wants so he hired me to leap into their volcano." *Joe Versus the Volcano*

Page 78 "If you think that Mick Jagger will still be doing the whole rock star thing at age fifty, well, then, you are sorely, sorely mistaken." *Almost Famous*

Solutions: Crypto Quotes

Page 80 "From the world's deepest ocean, From way down below, From down in the mud where the deep-divers go, From down in the mire and the muck and the murk, I might catch some fish who are all going, 'GLURK!'" "McElligot's Pool" — Dr. Seuss

Page 82 "I was asked to act when I couldn't act. I was asked to sing *Funny Face* when I couldn't sing, and to dance with Fred Astaire when I couldn't dance — and to do all kinds of things I wasn't prepared for. Then I tried like mad to cope with it."
— Audrey Hepburn

Page 84 "If you are lucky enough to have lived in Paris as a young man, then wherever you go for the rest of your life it stays with you, for Paris is a moveable feast."
— Ernest Hemingway

Solutions: Crypto Families

91

Page 7
Beatles Songs

"Love Me Do"
"Let It Be"
"Something"
"Yellow Submarine"
"No Reply"
"Twist and Shout"
"Helter Skelter"
"Come Together"
"Here Comes the Sun"
"Eight Days a Week"

Page 9
Italian Dishes

Spaghetti
Minestrone
Rigatoni
Gnocchi
Cannelloni
Panini
Ravioli
Linguini
Lasagna
Tortellini

Page 11
U.S. State Capitals

Carson City, Nevada
Sacramento, California
Tallahassee, Florida
Honolulu, Hawaii
Helena, Montana
Bismark, North Dakota
Baton Rouge, Louisiana
Indianapolis, Indiana
Montpelier, Vermont
Jefferson City, Missouri

Page 13
90s Best Picture Oscars®

Dances with Wolves
Forrest Gump
American Beauty
Unforgiven
Shakespeare in Love
Titanic
The Silence of the Lambs
The English Patient
Braveheart
Schindler's List

Solutions: Crypto Families

Page 15
Famous "Bills"
Billy the Kid
Billy Crystal
Bill Gates
Billy Joel
Bill Clinton
Bill Murray
Bill Cosby
Billie Holiday
Billy Bob Thornton
Bill Maher

Page 17
Constellations
Cassiopeia
Andromeda
Ursa Major
Orion
Pegasus
Perseus
Ursa Minor
Gemini
Hercules
Sagittarius

Page 19
Cartoon Characters
Bart Simpson
Yogi Bear
Huckleberry Hound
Fred Flintstone
Bugs Bunny
Mickey Mouse
Beavis and Butthead
Elmer Fudd
Bullwinkle J. Moose
Betty Boop

Page 21
Asian Food
Potstickers
Chow Mein
Pad Thai
Mu Shu Pancakes
Sushi
Spring Rolls
Won Tons
Sweet and Sour Soup
Teriyaki
Tempura

Page 23
'70s Best Picture Oscars®
Patton
The Godfather
The Sting
The Godfather Part II
Annie Hall
Rocky
The Deer Hunter
Kramer vs. Kramer
One Flew over the Cuckoo's Nest
The French Connection

Page 25
Broadway Hits
Phantom of the Opera
Cats
Les Miserables
Chicago
The Producers
Guys and Dolls
The King and I
The Lion King
West Side Story
Evita

Page 27
Oprah's Book Club Picks
The Poisonwood Bible
Songs in Ordinary Time
Daughter of Fortune
The Heart of a Woman
House of Sand and Fog
Gap Creek
The Pilot's Wife
She's Come Undone
White Oleander
One Hundred Years of Solitude

Page 29
James Bond Movies
A View to a Kill
Dr. No
From Russia with Love
Goldfinger
Die Another Day
Octopussy
Diamonds are Forever
The Living Daylights
Live and Let Die
The Spy Who Loved Me

Page 31
Earth's Islands
Mallorca
Puerto Rico
Oahu
Madagascar
Borneo
Greenland
Great Britain
Jamaica
Antigua
Bermuda

92

Solutions: Crypto Families

Page 33
Board Games
Candy Land
Clue
Monopoly
Trivial Pursuit
Twenty Questions
Scrabble
Balderdash
Chutes and Ladders
The Game of Life
Pictionary

Page 35
Types of Wine
Chianti
Pinot Noir
Sherry
Chablis
White Zinfandel
Cabernet Sauvignon
Merlot
Port
Chardonnay
Rose

Page 37
Al Pacino Movies
Scent of a Woman
Carlito's Way
Scarface
The Godfather
Glengarry Glen Ross
Author! Author!
Serpico

Sea of Love
Frankie and Johnny
Any Given Sunday

Page 39
Musicians Known by One Name
Madonna
Eminem
Cher
Sting
Beck
Bjork
Enya
Jewel
Bono
Sade

Page 41
Major League Baseball Hometowns
Pittsburgh
Houston
San Francisco
New York City
Detroit
Atlanta
St. Louis
Seattle
Cincinnati
Boston

Page 43
'60s Best Picture Oscars®
Lawrence of Arabia
The Apartment
West Side Story
Tom Jones
My Fair Lady
The Sound of Music
A Man for all Seasons
Oliver!
Midnight Cowboy
In the Heat of the Night

Page 45
Email Providers
www.earthlink.net
www.yahoo.com
www.aol.com
www.msn.com
www.netscape.com
www.hotmail.com
www.verizon.com
www.qwest.com
www.juno.com
www.compuserve.com

Page 47
Ice Cream Flavors
Mint Chip
French Vanilla
Chocolate
Coconut
Rocky Road
Strawberry
Cookies and Cream
Neapolitan
Butter Pecan
Coffee

Page 49
The Works Of Shakespeare
A Midsummer Night's Dream
Romeo and Juliet
Macbeth
Othello
The Comedy of Errors
Much Ado about Nothing
The Taming of the Shrew
Hamlet
The Merry Wives of Windsor
The Two Gentlemen of Verona

Solutions: Crypto Families

Page 51
Famous "Georges"
George Michael
George Clooney
George Harrison
Boy George
George W. Bush
George M. Cohan
George Foreman
George Lucas
Curious George
General George S. Patton

Page 53
Scary Movies
Nightmare on Elm Street
Scream
Halloween
The Sixth Sense
Fright Night
The Exorcist
The Texas Chainsaw Massacre
Psycho
Night of the Living Dead
The Mummy

Page 55
Cosmetics Manufacturers
Avon
Cover Girl
Loreal
Maybelline
Mary Kay
Lancome
Clinique
Chanel
Sephora
Urban Decay

Page 57
Children's Fairy Tales
Puss in Boots
The Princess and the Pea
Rumpelstiltskin
Thumbelina
Hansel and Gretel
Little Red Riding Hood
Tom Thumb
Beauty and the Beast
Jack and the Beanstalk
The Frog Prince

Page 59
Jewelry Gems
Opal
Garnet
Amethyst
Ruby
Diamond
Blue Topaz
Malachite
Jade
Amber
Onyx

Page 61
Diet Fads
South Beach Diet
Dr. Atkins' Diet
Mastering the Zone
Scarsdale Diet
Grapefruit Diet
Pritikin Diet
Eat Right for Your Type
Beverly Hills Diet
Cabbage Soup Diet
Neander-Thin: Eat Like a Caveman

Page 63
Elvis Presley Songs
"Love Me Tender"
"Heartbreak Hotel"
"Are You Lonesome Tonight?"
"Don't Be Cruel"
"Hound Dog"
"Jailhouse Rock"
"Suspicious Minds"
"Burning Love"
"A Little Less Conversation"
"All Shook Up"

Page 65
'80s Best Picture Oscars®
Ordinary People
Chariots of Fire
Gandhi
Terms of Endearment
Out of Africa
Amadeus
Platoon
The Last Emperor
Rain Man
Driving Miss Daisy

Page 67
Tropical Fruit
Banana
Papaya
Avocado
Mango
Pineapple
Guava
Passion Fruit
Pomegranate
Kiwi
Pawpaw

Page 69
Sesame Street Characters
Kermit the Frog
Grover
Big Bird
Oscar the Grouch
Elmo
Bert

Solutions: Crypto Families

Placido Flamingo
Ernie
Cookie Monster
Count von Count

Page 71
U.S. Presidents
Abraham Lincoln
George Washington
Grover Cleveland
Jimmy Carter
Gerald Ford
Zachary Taylor
Theodore Roosevelt
Chester A. Arthur
John F Kennedy
Ulysses S. Grant

Page 73
Julia Roberts Movies
Steel Magnolias
The Pelican Brief
My Best Friend's Wedding
Pretty Woman
Runaway Bride
Flatliners
Hook
Erin Brockovich
Sleeping with the Enemy
Mystic Pizza

Page 75
Chocolate Cravings
Pudding
Brownie
Ice Cream
Cake
Candy Bar
Truffle
Mousse
Hot Cocoa
Fondue
Hot Fudge

Page 77
Earth's Volcanoes
Mt. Kilimanjaro
Mt. Fuji
Mt. Etna
Mt. Vesuvius
Devil's Tower
Mt. St. Helens
Mt. Hood
Mt. Lassen
Paracutin
Krakatoa

Page 79
Rolling Stones Songs
"Ruby Tuesday"
"Beast of Burden"
"Brown Sugar"
"Start Me Up"
"Angie"
"Under My Thumb"
"Gimme Shelter"
"Honky Tonk Women"
"Sympathy for the Devil"
"(I Can't Get No) Satisfaction"

Page 81
Children's Authors
Maurice Sendak
J. K. Rowling
Lemony Snicket
Laura Ingalls Wilder
Dr. Seuss
Frank L. Baum
The Brothers Grimm
Madeleine L'Engle
Richard Scarry
Roald Dahl

Page 83
Audrey Hepburn Movies
Funny Face
Breakfast at Tiffany's
My Fair Lady
Sabrina
Love in the Afternoon
War and Peace
Always
Robin and Marian
Wait until Dark
Roman Holiday

Page 85
Countries & Their Capitals
Madrid, Spain
Paris, France
Brussels, Belgium
Beijing, China
Nairobi, Kenya
Manila, Philippines
Dublin, Ireland
New Delhi, India
Budapest, Hungary
Helsinki, Finland

About the Author

MARIA LLULL is a longtime creator and solver of word puzzles. She first honed her puzzling and gaming skills as a University Games staff member and now combines her successful career as a freelance writer with daily chess matches against her 8-year-old son Zack.